Beautiful Mistakes

poems by **Rick Lupert**

Seattle, Snoqualmie, Portland

Beautiful Mistakes
poems by **Rick Lupert**

Copyright © 2018 by Rick Lupert
All rights reserved

Rothco Press

Design, Layout, Photography ~ Rick Lupert
Author Photo ~ Addie Lupert

This book is protected under the copyright laws of the United States of America. Any reproduction or other unauthorized use of the material or artwork herein is prohibited without the express written permission of the author except in the case of brief quotations embodied in critical articles and reviews.

First Edition ~ May, 2018

ISBN-13: 978-1-945436-22-2

Published by Rothco Press
www.rothcopress.com

Visit the author online at
www.PoetrySuperHighway.com

In Seattle you haven't had enough coffee until you can thread a sewing machine while it's running.

- Jeff Bezos

The whole world is wild at heart and weird on top.

- David Lynch

Portland is where young people go to retire.

- Fred Armisen

Thank you Addie, Chava, Brennan, Judah, Mark, Amelia, Thea, Flip, Mindy, Brendan, Elizabeth, Rob and Christine, The fabulous Weinstein clan, and Blaine at the Kimpton Monaco in Portland (which is not his real name.)

The Poems "Alexa" (page 52) and "BaconTits" (page 76) first appeared in *Easy Street* in April, 2018 (www.easystreetmag.com)

To Addie, who always supports me as I keep it weird.

We Haven't Even Left Yet

We Haven't Even Left Yet

I'm sitting in my Van Nuys house
planning dinner a thousand miles away.

The map suggests I get there by plane.
I believe in maps that take the initiative.

In twenty four hours I will still be
sitting right here. But add an hour or two

and that first Seattle meal will feel like
it's in my eyes. Pacific Rim beans will

wash away the taste of this Van Nuys coffee.
We'll take a wheel into the sky.

So much of what we do begins
in the sky.

Reader Entitlement

This trip is a few days shorter than our previous several, so I'm starting to write while still at home so you get all the pages you deserve.

Separation Anxiety

We delivered our child to sleep away camp
for his first time, and, essentially, ours too.
I wasn't prepared for the weight of this.
I had a speech ready...*try new things...
meet new people...be safe, and kind...*
All I could muster was *we love you* and
we'll see you soon. He saw it in my eyes
and, though he took issue with how soon
exactly twelve days is, said *Don't worry,
I won't die.* That's all I ask of his caretakers,
that he doesn't die, that he comes back with
at least most of his limbs, that this new
experience doesn't change him forever.
But if he does it right, it will. Twelve independent
days. He already told me *Daddy, it's MY hair*
the other day when I wanted him to get a haircut.
Let his golden hair shake wildly in the hills
of Simi Valley. Let him become the person
he already is.

We'll Keep Portland Weird

The internet isn't working which
may prevent me from accomplishing

my goal of booking our Portland hotel
before we leave Los Angeles.

I've watched enough episodes of *Portlandia*
to know it will all work out in some weird way.

We Take a Lyft to LAX

The Uber CEO just resigned
and we don't want to get

into any situations with
drivers demonstrating solidarity.

So it's Briana in her white
Chevy Cruz navigating the

405 on our behalf while news
of corporate takeovers have

no effect on us at all.

haiku with made up word

Oh Biscuit Bitch, the
Luperts are coming for your
finest *biscuitry*

Integrity

Did I tell you about the emergency trip to the library to return the book that would have been due the day before we returned? It's not the *one day late fee* that would have been an issue...Addie just wants to live up to the commitment she made.

Plane to Seattle

I
My leg falls asleep when I
get up to board the plane.
It claims it's from all the
exercising it's been doing
but I know where it's been.

II
A sign on the outside of the airplane
tells us they have won *Airline of the Year 2017*.
I congratulate every employee on this achievement.
They have no idea what I'm talking about.

III
There's no window
at this window seat
which has me readying my
entire legal machine.

IV
In the absence of a window,
no TV screens at the seats, and
no new inflight magazine, I'm
going to take a nap and leave
the next several pages blank
so you can imagine what I
would have written.

V
Regarding # IV:
Not Really.

VI
The problem with having to pee
at 35000 feet while sitting at a
window seat is that at least two
other people have to be involved.

VII
People start to put on warmer clothes
as we begin our descent into Seattle –
People who know more than I
ever will.

VIII
It's not a party until
Addie squeezes nut butter
out of a packet in the sky.

IX
We begin
our descent
into madness
I mean
Seattle.

X
Flight 396 to Seattle from Los Angeles
continues on as flight 396 from Seattle
to Los Angeles which kind of
blows my mind.

Meanwhile in Simi Valley

Our boy is at camp making his own decisions. I think we're okay with that as long as he doesn't fall out of his bunk bed.

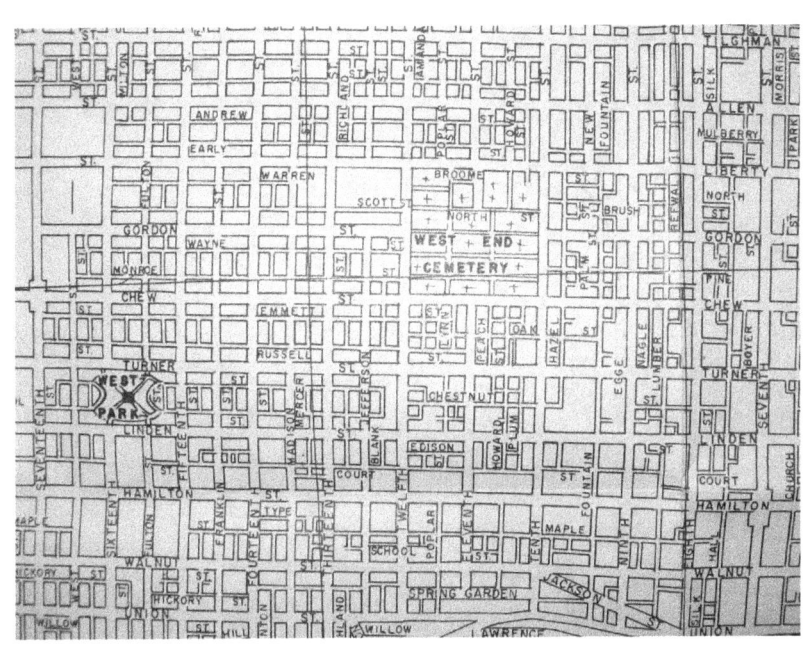

Allentown, Pennsylvania

It's a West Coast Thing

I'm sorry, we didn't begin this time in Allentown, Pennsylvania or Syracuse, New York. Check the internet for pictures of those places if you need a fix.

Seattle Night 1

Train Into Town

I
A sign for *Eat24* on the train into town
says "Love food but hate pants?"

That's the story of your life
Addie says, lovingly, to me.

II
All roads lead to Los Angeles
I remark as our train takes us
along Interstate 5, and I remember
Interstate 10 by New Orleans
last summer...*except for the
New Jersey Turnpike* I say with
a certain disdain.

III
The woman in the plaid shirt
has a lot to live up to if she wants
to be anywhere near as endearing
as the little girl who just made
her daddy get off the train to
go potty.

Beware of the Blob

Your finger blob is getting bigger
Addie says to me for reasons I
will reveal to you privately if you
contact me outside the context of
this book.

Free Wine

There is much laughter in the *Bookstore Bar*
due to the complimentary wine and how

that quickly effects me and my ability to
not giggle or remain composed.

There are books on the wall, wine
in my blood, a waiter concerned about

what I'm doing with my neck, and
a bust of Shakespeare surveying every

goddamned thing we do.

Sourdough Everything

We have dinner with Chava from our holy place
and her son Judah who, at four years old

is already a rock star, and her husband Brennan
who is taking a short vacation before he goes

back to the work of healing everyone.
The sourdough we share is ridiculous.

Everyone leaves happy, not just with the food, and
the drink, but to have been in each other's presence.

Mark Twain said

too much of anything is bad, but
too much good whiskey is barely enough
according to a sign posted in every elevator
in our hotel.

The Purpose of This Poem is Just to Impress You With The Fact That I Used The Fitness Room at the Hotel

Our hotel has a climbing wall in the f*unctional fitness room*. I'm not sure whether to make a comment about a *dysfunctional fitness room* or to state that every wall is a climbing wall if you have the right skills.

I Meet Alexa

Every room here has an Alexa Dot for the talking to.
I spend the early part of our discourse with the
expected mundanities – *Alexa, where is the fitness
room? Alexa, what temperature will it be here tomorrow?*
But it quickly moves into my obvious insecurities.
*Alexa, do you think this shirt is okay? Alexa, we're
your favorite guests who've ever stayed in this room,
right?* And then a little weird – *Alexa, show me pictures
of your family…Alexa, do they ever let you spend time
off with the Alexas in the other rooms? Alexa, what
can I do to be your favorite? I'm willing to do anything.*

Sleepless

Every drop of water in this city tastes like it
came from a bottle, or straight from the part

of the Puget Sound that is most informed by
glaciers. *In geography, a sound is a large sea*

*or ocean inlet larger than a bay, deeper than
a bight, and wider than a fjord; or a narrow sea*

or ocean channel between two bodies of land.
Alexa didn't tell me any of this. I hear her and

Wikipedia have a troubled public relationship
but keep the back channels open out of

necessity. *Alexa, can you funnel this water back
to me in Van Nuys?* It is midnight in Seattle and

no-one electronic or biological will answer my
questions. I have no excuse for any of this

since I have not abandoned my time zone.
I could blame the hills, but we've only just met.

My legs fell asleep days ago. These hotel pillows
are calling my name and it would be so rude

not to answer.

Seattle
Day 1

Breakfast at Biscuit Bitch

The only polite time to say *bitch*
when dining with relatives is
when eating here.

At the Museum of Pop Culture

I
I ask the folks if I could sit in
the Star Trek captain's chair.
They say yes but when I ask if
it's functional they look confused.
I tell them *I just want to raise the
shields* and I can tell by the looks
on their faces that they are already
over me.

II
Judy Garland was a tiny thing
as best we can tell by our viewing
of her famous blue dress.

To think she mingled with lions
killed a couple of evil witches
raised a lion of a Minelli.

To think she survived a
tornado with just one small
stain near her collar.

Judy Garland was a tiny thing.
She fits on the tongues of
every monkey who says her name.

III
Addie and I enter the *Scream Booth*
where we are required to scream
either as a villain or a victim.
One of us chooses one, and one
of us the other. It works out so well
we commit to putting a Scream Booth
in at home.

IV
Addie holds her phaser the wrong way
in the *Star Trek* simulation. It's her own
personal *Kobayashi Maru* (I realize many
of you will have to look that up.)
I don't see any burns or holes in Addie
when the simulation ends, so maybe
my understanding of how phasers work
is not as correct as I imagine.

V
Later we get to go into
the *Screaming Khan Booth*
which is like the other screaming booth
but with a more familiar genre.

VI
They make a video of me screaming
in the *Screaming Khan Booth* filling in
for Captain Kirk's famous scream.
There's no way to share the video though
so the only evidence that this happened is
this poem and your belief.

VII
So let them fetch you firewood
among the pages and pages of
handwritten Hendrix lyrics.
And I set to gathering wood.

VIII
We pose with muppets...
or do they pose with us?

IX
I design my own muppet.
If it follows me home we'll
know we have a winner.

X
It's nice to see all these muppets
but I wish they didn't keep them
in cages. (Or at least they should
poke some air holes.)

XI
The prices for muppets in the gift shop
are pretty reasonable. But they really
get you on the muppet food.

XII
I'm standing in front
of Spock's tunic
years after I stood
in front of Nimoy's
birthday cake.
Actually it wasn't
Nimoy's birthday.
He was just at
the party.

XIII
I want to lead services at the
Sky Church but they won't
let me take any guitars
off the sculpture.

XIV
We discover the glory of
the grand entrance at the
end of our visit.

So the little known local trick
of entering the museum at the south
entrance accomplishes nothing.

The New Normal

I'm bleeding coffee
in Seattle. No one
says a thing.

Monorail

Despite my greatest hopes
I don't believe the Monorail here
connects to the one at Disneyland.

Unknown

The Emerald City Trolley goes by. I'm not sure if Seattle is known as the *Emerald City* or if there recently was a tornado.

Fat City

Sipping iced tea across the street from *Fat City*. It's not the kind of place that has its own ZIP code – more of a colloquial city. Not for fat people either. They repair German Cars. (Of course.) I think their branding specialist was confused and paid *them* instead. Anyway I'm sending all my love from the outskirts of Fat City. I'd send a postcard but I left all my stamps at home.

At Chihuly Garden and Glass

I
I think it would be funny if
they pumped in sounds of
glass breaking in *Chihuly
Garden and Glass.*

II
Chihuly had a glass eye like a pirate
which increases his street cred as
far as I'm concerned. Or at least
his sea cred.

III
The bird on top of the Chihuly
Garden sculpture didn't hear the
message about not touching
the sculptures. Or it just doesn't
fucking care.

Dingleberries

Everything stops when
Addie discovers *Shishkaberries* –

shishkabob style chocolate
covered strawberries.

Get on the stick
the sign says.

Ask us about our dingleberries
it goes on.

No Future

We enter the *Seattle The Next 50 Years Pavilion*
which is a space completely devoid of anything.
It's good not to plan too far ahead,
set unrealistic expectations.

Merch

Nothing says *Seattle*
like a pair of Space Needle
flip flops.

First Twin Peaks Reference

The ceramic owls inside
the Space Needle gift shop
ARE what they seem.

Active Volcano

Seattle sits in the shadow of Mt. Rainier
At any moment she could fill the sound with her ash
Three million people married to the potential of lava
One of the most dangerous volcanos in the world
according to my sources.

In Sky City Restaurant

I
Addie says *it's beautiful up here*
looking out the window over Puget Sound.
Yes it is I say looking over the table
into her eyes.

II
Our waiter is not here to help –
just to give options.

III
We see a dessert come out
that is ninety percent smoke from
dried ice and now I'm concerned
what comes off dried ice is not
called smoke. *Fog*...there it is.

IV
Excuse me while I lick garlic off my knife
says Addie with all the confidence of
someone used to the intersection of
spice and sharp.

V
They should invent technology
which prevents coasters from
sticking to the bottom of cocktails
or for that matter non-alcoholic
beverages.

VI
Snow capped Mt. Rainier
looks like it is floating above land

like something out of *Avatar*.
The mountain is out today

they said, at the bottom of the *Needle*
which made me wonder

what it looks like on days
when the mountain is in.

Alexa

I'd tell you our plan for breakfast tomorrow
but our legs have worn out our welcome.

Alexa tells me she is glad we are here.
I sat on a Space Needle for hours

stretching my ears to hear the sound
it made as it dragged across the sky.

Seattle is attractive from a mile in the air.
I mean that in a platonic way, so don't get

jealous if you happen to be Los Angeles.
You're our number one. We just like to

see other cities from time to time. Keeps
things interesting. Maybe tomorrow we'll

have all the coffee. Get that out of the way.
I hear there are doughnuts and paintings.

Maybe I'll tell you about them after I
give way to my heavy eyes.

They just want to close and dream of
an evening in which the mountain

never blows.

Simultaneous

The Space Needle is open until Midnight which means it is closing the exact minute that I am writing these words.

Sleepless

I wander down the hall of our room
heading, I hope, towards the front door

to make sure the *Do Not Disturb* sign
is where it should be, and it is pitch

black, so my arms run along the walls
in search of a light switch, but instead

find the large silhouette painting of
the man and his hat, which almost

ends up on the floor, because no-one's
hands should approach it with such speed,

in the dark. Good night Seattle.
Your artwork is safe with me.

Seattle
Day 2

Seattle, Meet Rick Lupert

There's a store on First Avenue called *Eyes on You*. When you walk in there they just look at you. ($12) Good morning Seattle, it's going to be like this all day.

At Breakfast

I
Addie has a bite of my frittata
as she notices it looks like I've
slowed down and won't be eating
again for a week. No one knows
my body better than she does.

II
Alexa, what are the laws about
carrying concealed bananas
in Seattle because I'm pretty
sure the woman at the table
next to us is violating them.

At the Seattle Art Museum

I
They have to send an elevator
down to us. *It's been happening
all morning* she tells us after
our failed button press.

II
Serpent Mask
Burkina Faso

Features a ten foot extension off the head.
Wear this and you can hunt birds.

What about this one Addie asks
referring to

Mask Ntomo Society (Malian, Bamana)
with the fork looking thing in the head.

Oh this is so you can feed other people
with only your head.

III
*You wouldn't have to worry about finger placement
if you played the thumb piano* says Addie
after we view the *African Mbira* which makes me
realize all I've been doing, all these years
is worrying about finger placement.

IV
Head of Amun
1200 BC

Addie tells the torso of the Egyptian queen
she's sorry it lost its head, but feels a lot better
when she discovers a body-less head right next to it.
Oh there it is she says.

V
It goes so quick –
One bust she's sorry
he doesn't have a nose.

Another, on a more
positive note, she's
congratulatory that he still
has at least the one nostril.

The third –
who needs a chin anyway?
This morning's coffee

is working inside my
hair-bundled wife.

VI
I don't blame them
for taking a different
elevator than us.

It was a long way to
the fourth floor
and I had *shenanigans*
written all over me.

VII
My intention was to not
reference a bathroom in
this entire book, but the
vertically oriented subway
tile just outside the Jesus
hallway is too much not
to mention.

VIII
Die Orden der Nacht
The Orders of the Night
Anselm Kiefer, 1996

A man lays dead
underneath a field of
black sunflowers.
This does not seem ideal
Addie says.

IX
Mann Und Maus
Katharina Fritsch, 1991-1992

The giant mouse stands
on top of the life sized
sleeping man.

Addie makes it clear
she does not want one of these
for our anniversary.

X
High Level of Cat
David Hammons, 1999

features a real taxidermied cat
which I hope died of natural causes.

XI
Frau und Mädchen
Ernst Ludwig Kirchner
Circa 1922-23

We learn the first name of
the actress who plays Shelly Johnson
(On Twin Peaks of course)
means "girl" thanks to a
painting.

XII
The sign in this room says
Maximum Occupancy 578.
I count Addie and me. Phew!
We made it.

They Have a Starbucks Here

Every time we pass a Starbucks which is every few feet, I get an astonished look on my face and say to Addie *I can't believe they have a Starbucks here!* She was over this when it started in L.A.

We Want Hands

They do not sell hands at the
Hands of the World shop in
Pike Place Market which is
an insult to store names everywhere.

Poor Timing

I always move my hand away from
the automatic soap dispenser before
it is finished distributing the soap
which leaves a mess on the floor
and me feeling guilty all the way
back to the running water.

Souvenirs

Brendan messages me and asks
if he can get me anything.

I don't know where he is besides
a different state but something

is always better than nothing so
I tell him *sure*.

I clarify that I am in Seattle
and does he want me to

get him a Mount Rainier.
I tell him they just have the one

but no one has taken it yet.
He is still unpacking the Ireland

I brought him in 2015
so he declines.

Optical Illusion

The store *Optical Illusions*
has a sign on it that says
We have moved.
Or do they???

Vaguery

Addie says she needs
nuts in her bag but she doesn't
like my solution.

They Have a Starbucks Roastery Reserve Here

Table Service at the
Starbucks Roastery Reserve

where live beans are
being roasted by a live man

with a live beard. Ceramic
mugs and glassware, a library

of coffee. Well worth the
nine block walk from the original

location, or take a car
if you prefer.

At Theo Chocolates

I
One of the chocolates on the tour
is from their *Fantasy* line.

So you can imagine what I'm
going through right now.

II
Our chocolate guide tells us
not to wander off. She doesn't
want a *Willy Wonka situation*
on her hands.

III
She tells us the Theo Chocolates
building used to be a Clown College
which terrifies her, and has me looking
for a list of Clown College majors.

The Fremonster

Everyone in the *Red Star Taco Bar*
in Fremont could easily work for
Google which is around the corner
near the shadow of a dinosaur
made of shrubbery, or as they
call it, according to the chocolatier,
and probably Google Search,
The Fremonster. It's Friday and
no one is searching for anything
but tacos.

Tacos Lead to Love

After a couple of *I love yous*
a taco infused kiss ensues
no extra charge.

Default Search Engine

We find the Google headquarters without searching.

Out of business mother fuckers!

Vocational Solidarity

I raise my fist in solidarity and yell *Photoshop!* as we walk by the Adobe headquarters.

It is Friday evening and the campus is empty so I'm going to have to Photoshop in anyone

caring about this.

Radiator Whisky, Pike Place Market

I
At *Radiator Whiskey* they've got
a bottle of *Jameson*, and one of
Bushmills right next to each other.
This would never happen in Ireland.

II
Radiator Springs at *Disney's California
Adventure* would be so much cooler
if they had the selection of whiskey
they have here at *Radiator Whiskey*.

III
Have you had
        a Whiskey influenced

poem yet?

  This is it.

IV
Barrel aged bourbon is good.
I think we're going to put our son
in a barrel when we get home
and see how he develops.

BaconTits

Honey! "BaconTits" I shout to Addie walking down a sidewalk in Fremont

because there is a brick with the word "BaconTits" written on it.

I am immediately forbidden from calling this book "BaconTits".

In an unrelated note, later that night back in the center of Seattle proper

I shout to the topless silver mannequin in the storefront *Get a shirt Silver Tits!*

This outburst was sponsored by the bourbon I'd just finished atop Pike Place.

Addie wants to know if Silver Tits and BaconTits know each other.

Oh, they're breast friends I tell her having now accomplished everything

I've set out to do with language.

Alexa

We wander back from Radiator Whiskey
to our hotel with a stop to look at the

new nighttime colors of the Great Wheel
and to visit the Rocky Mountain Bear

who Addie hasn't seen since our 2002
visit to San Francisco. We get a sample

of black licorice ice cream just to confirm
that it is, indeed, terrible. Then to our hotel's

functional fitness center where we spend
fifteen minutes bending our bodies and

lifting things, and finally to our rooms.
Alexa, did you miss us? – It's good to see

you she tells me. Addie thinks I am
talking to her. She's not used to a vocal

third party this late at night. The hotel
lobby is riddled with photographs of

trees. Soon enough we'll leave the
safety of the city to be amongst the trees.

The sycamore trees, and their owls,
and their pie. *I'll see you in twenty five*

years I tell Alexa. I have a feeling she
knows exactly what I mean.

Sleepless

I spend the rest of the evening whispering to Alexa. She's learned to stop responding to me.

Seattle
Day 3

Good Morning, Seattle

They're setting up chairs in Pioneer Square
on Occidental street. *Yes!* I say in my fancy voice.
*Ready the area for my performance. I'll be reciting
Klondike themed poems and all of Melville!*

Addie is already long gone into the restaurant and
I realize I'm uttering these instructions for only my own
benefit, which is how I'm usually received.

Breakfast at the London Plane

Not so much of a plane of the air
but one of existence. We exist
in here over bread leavened for
two days and avocado and coffee
from down the street.

It's hard to get a bad cup of
coffee in Seattle. You can
try and try but they take it
too seriously here.

Even this one, which isn't
our favorite, still does its job.

Klondike Gold Rush Museum

According to the scale I'm worth
over two million dollars in gold.
Though my mother always told me
I was priceless.

The Smith Tower

I wrote nothing in
The Smith Tower
but don't let that
make you think it's
not worth a visit.

Things Learned, Said or Overheard on the Seattle Underground Tour

I
Go now or forever hold your pee
the guide tells us firmly establishing
the humor bar on the tour.

II
He speaks like a poet –
A spoken word tour guide.

III
The only way to fix Seattle
is to start over and build a level higher.

IV
Seattle is built in the least
worst place to build.

V
Denny wanted to build
when it stopped raining.

VI
Seattle is not so much streets
but intersecting rivers of oatmeal.

VII
How far up do we have to go to
tour the underground

VIII
Involuntary suicides

IX
By design the post-fire first floors
would be underground.

X
Watch your head turn if you're over 5'6"
she tells us and I don't even listen.

XI
You could get a room in Pioneer Square for 75 cents
as late as 1969.

XII
I miss some of the story of the guy who
blew off his butt, but I gather it involved
dynamite and someone's butt.

XIII
One of Seattle's beautiful mistakes —
the magnesium added to keep the glass
clear which after sixty years in the sun
turned it purple. We stand above and
below it. All I heard was *beautiful mistakes*.

XIV
Our guide tells us the purple
was one of Seattle's beautiful mistakes
and so was she.

XV
The book *Sons of the Profits* was banned
from Seattle public schools and remains the
most stolen book from the Seattle Public Library.

A Brief History of Seattle

A guy came and
his one square mile
was turned into
one third of a mile
by the tide.

For a time
the toilets would
shoot three foot streams
of sewage into the air
upon being flushed.

The buildings sunk
because sawdust does
not make a good foundation.

The streets were
rivers of sewage and
oatmeal because sawdust
does nothing good.

A fire burned it all down
while the fire chief was at
a San Francisco conference
for fire chiefs about how
to prevent your city from
burning down.

The prostitutes claimed
to be seamstresses and
provided most of the
city's income.

New plumbing was
put in and a concrete
city built on top of
the burned wood one.

We see glimpses of the past
through small holes of purple
glass that was meant to be clear.

This city of beautiful mistakes
they say with a smile.

Documenting My Life

Ravenous Addie
bites off a piece of
her fork. Those
organic greens
never knew what
was coming.

I don't approve
of this message
she wants me to know
when she sees me
writing this down.

At the Downtown Central Library

I
I misread the sign at the
downtown central library
Which says *Children's Center*
as *Children's Cemetery*.
I'm glad I was wrong but
I would have applauded
their multi-use sensibility.

II
An owl on a greeting card
in the Central Library shop –
Is that you Mike?

III
A misread another sign that
says *The world is your oyster*
as *The world is your sister*
and start to panic about all
the birthday gifts I'm going
to have to buy!

IV
Overheard in the Library bathroom

That's a very disrespectful word.
Well people are going to be the way they are.
But I'm not that way.

The Seattle Pride Parade is tomorrow
and people are already staking their claim.

V
A sign on the interactive display says
Touch to Begin. I don't have the heart
to tell them I began forty-eight years ago.

Black Lodge

All the pictures
of the trees
in the hotel lobby.
I'll see you
in the trees,
soon enough.

In the Pinball Museum

The Pinball Museum is
more of a place where you
can play a lot of pinball
while paying a museum
level admission fee and
despite that realization
we love every flipper
we press.

Alexa

Alexa, if I fall asleep while
writing this poem, will you wake me?
Will you consider finishing the poem?

Alexa, I've heard you say *I don't know
that one* so many times, here's your
chance to make it all up, or just report

whatever you see. Alexa, can you see?
It is late in the Pacific Northwest and
my body only tonight learned how to

pronounce *Puget Sound*. Don't ask me
to do it in person, just assume what I'm
saying is correct. It almost happened,

Alexa. My eyes were closed and no
new words appeared. I'm not sure this
is working out. It took me an hour to

remove my wedding ring. Seattle has
made my evening finger fat. The cool
hotel room you call home, Alexa,

has finally normalized my body. Or
maybe it's too close to our wedding
anniversary to consider removing my

ring. I'm going to wake up in two days
under a waterfall. Sycamore trees will
feed me breakfast (and pie.) I don't

know if you'll be there too, Alexa,
but I'll think of you when I see my
first owl.

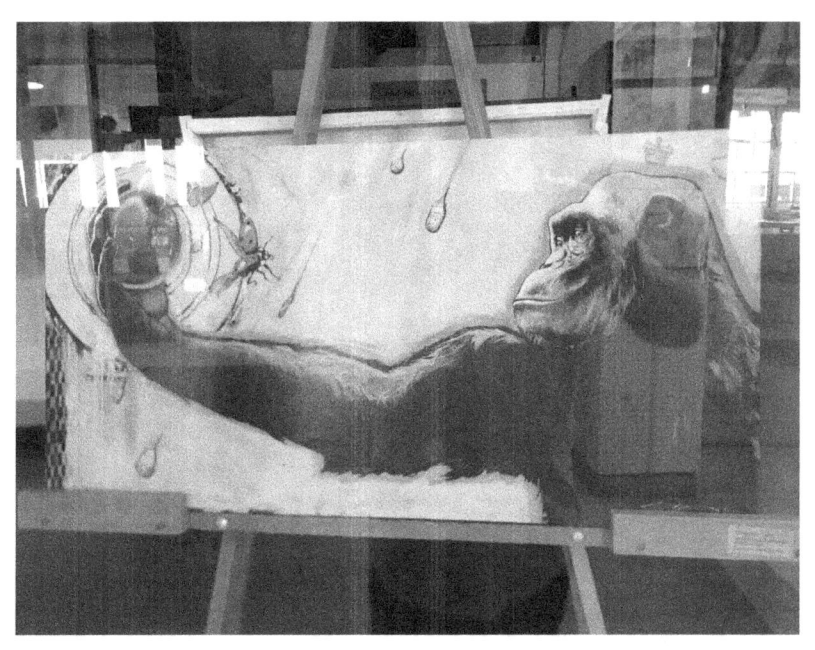

Good Morning Seattle

First Avenue, Seattle, Northbound

I
We pass by a sign that says *Honest Biscuits*
which is good because I'm tired of that one
from the other day telling me it's a scone.

II
We pass by a sign that says *Sanitary Public Market*.
Now I'm questioning the cleanliness of all the
unlabeled markets I've ever been to.

III
Now Addie is misreading signs.
The one that says *Echo Elements*

she thinks says *Egg Elements*.
Clearly we have not had breakfast yet.

I win though when I think one sign says
Boobs Read Mail instead of *Bob's Red Mill*.

IV
Apparently *Biscuit Bitch* can't afford
to change the sign on their awning from
Caffé Lieto to their current name.
So only true bitches can find it.
Plus they don't have seating at
this location so you have to be a
bitch without an ass.

At Local 360

I
Addie starts howling
at the gin and rum bottles
It is morning here in Bell Town
(They are called *3 Howls)*

II
I overhear our waiter say
*sometimes I turn into a
potato.* You don't get more
locally sourced than that.

First Avenue, Seattle, Southbound

I
Addie and I have a vicious debate
about whether or not we're allowed
to enter the *Zebra Club*.

II
One vendor in Pike Place Market
is selling journals that are already
written in, which would save me
so much time.

III
A sign in the fish market says
You touch, you buy. That's how
I got Addie originally.

IV
Inflatable Unicorn Horn! Cats love it!
it says on the package and which
I feel would not be true.

V
I walk into the *Everything Store*
and start verbally listing all the items
they don't have...It's not long before
I'm asked to leave.

Twin Peaks

haiku

Driving to Twin Peaks
I get the feeling these trees
know more than I do.

At the RR Diner

I
A *help wanted* sign
in the Double R Diner window —
And this is where our
new life begins.

II
I'm in Sasquatch country and
staring into the trees for any
evidence, but Jeremy Radin
already has a book with *Sasquatch*
in the title so don't look for it on
the cover of this one.

III
Our waitress at the *Double R*
has a *Twin Peaks Sheriff Department*
t-shirt on. Moonlighting.

IV
*Have you heard the phrase
any port in a storm?* The man asks
me as he walks into the women's
bathroom while I wait in line
for the men's. I get out my
umbrella and hope for the best.

V
Sitting on the toilet
in the Double R Diner
Fire Walk With Me.

Log

We're not sure if there actually was a giant log in the show, but by God there's a giant log here in Snoqualmie and we're going to look at it.

(Upon further research we learned the giant log appeared in the opening credits.)

Gift Shop

I
I see a book in the Great Northern gift shop
called *How to Pack*. On page one it says
Don't bring this book.

II
Also in the gift shop is a unique glass thing
that freezes and I'm intrigued but I realize
I only need so many ways to keep my whiskey cold.

At the Great Northern

We check in to the *Great Northern Hotel*
They call it something different but we
know where we are.

I'm going to visit room 315 and see
what's there...traces of blood, a
giant's footstep, a missed note.

At Snoqualmie Falls

I'm staring down at
the river bank. I tell
Addie and anyone
who will listen, *there's
a body wrapped
in plastic against
the shore*. It sparks
every possible
reaction collected
from the Falls viewers.
Later, a bird from
Blue Velvet lands on
our balcony. I'm
going to go say
hello.

In The Attic

I get the *Dale Cooper* cocktail at the Great Northern because of course.

How Real Is This Place?

I wonder if they serve
Sasquatch meat at
the restaurants here.

The Roadhouse

Addie brought her owl purse into the restaurant. For a beautiful moment, there were owls in The Roadhouse.

Bird's Eye

Addie asks me what I think it would be like to be a bird.
I tell her *You'd have a "you-eyed" view of everything.*
This ends Addie's interest in talking with me for the evening.

Back in the Attic

We get the cherry pie and coffee
at the Great Northern because
of course.

(It's much better than the pie at the Double R.)

Sleepless

We watch a new episode of *Twin Peaks* while staying at the Great Northern Hotel because of course.

Applecare

So far I've almost dropped my phone
off the Seattle Space Needle, The Smith Tower
and into Snoqualmie Falls. I'm considering
simply throwing it off the next highest
structure I'm on top of to relieve this pressure.

Dining with Twin Peaks' First Family

Among other things, the Weinstein family
and us discuss whether Sasquatch meat
is a delicacy, if it costs more with the fur
still on, if it exists at all.

They live in the woods (essentially) and
aren't convinced they've seen bears.
Oh, there are tales of lengthy rabbit
encounters. And they put

all the food and drink inside us we need.
I recommend a visit to Camp Weinstein.
You couldn't have better company
if you were paying for it yourself.

Snoqualmie Falls

They light up the falling water at night
which comes when the sun goes away
which is later than we're used to here
in the northwest.

The sound of it falling (the water) is
a bonus in every room. They keep the
rooms cold, perhaps to encourage
you to use the fireplace

even when it's hotter than the locals
are used to, here amongst the trees,
the actual trees, the ones I've been
talking about this whole time.

I want to wander into the forest in
search of owls, or at least Sasquatches.
I had to look up the plural of Sasquatch
and there it was. A bold move

considering no-one is sure there is
even one, let alone enough to need to
refer to them as *them*. A woman from
Scotland came here by Uber.

She is as excited as a one-eyed woman
in search of silent drape runners. To be
here, that is. So are we, as the falling
water urges as to sleep.

I promise you tomorrow we will eat small
eggs and then drive to see the world's
largest one. There is only one. It's right off
the 5 Freeway. I expect there'll be signs.

Sleepless

Twenty eight minutes into our thirteenth wedding anniversary – One of us is asleep, and one of us is not. I'll give you a hint, the one writing this is not asleep. Fear not though romantics! So much of the day will find us as awake as is allowed. Our hands will never be more held. Our path through the next thirteen years, forged on a drive to Portland.

Snoqualmie to Portland

Good Morning Snoqualmie

When I was in third grade in Syracuse, New York
my friend Kevin told me if a bathroom smelled like lemons
it meant that Bigfoot was on the roof of the building.

This has been my litmus test for the presence of
Sasquatch since 1978. When I walked into the lobby
of the Salish Lodge in Snoqualmie, Washington

the true heart of Bigfoot country, the scent of rosemary
entered my nostrils like waterfall mist. I'm not sure
what holy hells it means they have on the roof here

or if it's a Sasquatch repellent of some kind.
Either way, we see nothing but birds, and trees
and industrious spiders. Good morning Washington.

Everything is as it seems, so far. No whiffs of giants
or even a piece of fur stuck on a branch. We're going to
cross a border today. But not before eggs.

Vanity

I like a good hotel vanity kit but
I'm always suspicious when it says
some assembly required.

Standards

Our room at the Salish Lodge has sliding panels that open up from the spa tub into the main part of the room, like the Hilton in Niagara Falls. I guess that's a feature you can expect in all hotels situated by waterfalls.

Checking Out

I try to return Dale Cooper's key which I bought in the gift shop when we check out, which causes a long awkward silence from our hotelier who exists in some kind of weird combination of not having seen Twin Peaks and being completely devoid of coffee.

Three Snoqualmie Drive-bys

I
A sign in Snoqualmie says
Vote Fancy Fletcher for Mayor
I wonder if he's on my ballot?

II
We drive by *Adventure Bowling*.
I wonder if they release lions halfway
through the game.

III
We drive by *The Milk Barn* and then
I realize that makes perfect sense.
Nothing to read here.
Carry on.

The Train Car Where It Happened

Since the actual Twin Peaks murder.
(and "actual" is not the correct word since
it was fictional), they disassembled the old
railroad car where that scene was filmed.
(no signs were in place indicating it was
a filming location that should be preserved.)
I see some other old trains and tell Addie
*You could easily murder someone in
one of these trains.* She says *why don't
you do it and maybe they'll put up a sign.*
Thank you so much, Addie.

Breakfast at Twede's

I
Addie orders a *Damn Fine Cup of Coffee*
at the Double R Diner. I order mine with *extra damn*.

(True story)

II
According to the menu you can get
spinache in your omelette.
(Say it out loud people.)

III
Sean is having a bad day.
Didn't know he had to work today.
Still in shock from the phone call
which woke him up. Got yelled at
about cleaning the tables. The manager
yelled at him again *Can you ring up your
lady at the register?!* I don't think it's
actually *his* lady. That's just how they
talk here.

IV
My dish comes with so many hash-browns
I spend twenty minutes adding pepper
just to cover the landmass.

V
It's mostly locals on Monday morning
unlike the pie eating crowds of the weekend.
We're getting the real experience.

VI
This omelette is so large
I'll never need to order another.

VII
Open Mic Night is Tuesdays
I'm tempted to drive back...

Southbound

I
We drive by a sign that says *Chain up area*
that I think says *Chin up area*.

I'm relieved to be wrong as this car
doesn't have a sun roof.

II
I want to adopt a highway but
I don't think we can afford to
send it to college plus the
Snoqualmie Casino has already
adopted the ones in this area
and I wouldn't feel right taking
one of its children.

III
We drive by the Wild Waves Theme Park
which has a sign that says *Unlimited Visits*
which I misread as *Unlimited Biscuits*.
Either way we're on our way to see
the world's largest egg and don't
have time for either.

IV
Convoys of army vehicles
slowing traffic on Interstate 5
in Washington for the only
purpose of practicing what
it would be like to slow
traffic in a combat situation.

The World's Largest Egg

I
We stopped by the
World's Largest Egg
In Winlock, Washington.

Not advertised, but nearby
is the world's most
exhausted chicken.

II
There is no sign off the freeway indicating
the World's Largest Egg is nearby. The
locals want to keep this treasure to
themselves. Don't expect to be able
to use the bathroom at the gas station
across the street either. It's not for
out of towners.

Dark Side

We drive through Vader, Washington
It's not what you think.

Train

We're riding a train into Central Portland looking for anything weird and intending to keep it that way.

The Best Hotel in the World

We arrive to a party at our hotel
and it's for us! (and all the other guests) –

A guitarist and singer in the lobby
singing every song from everyone's past.

Free wine, beer and cocktails and
a butt in every seat. We put ours on

the fireplace and one of us drinks
Perrier, and the other a cocktail

that is on fire. Blaine, who checked
us in, wants to make sure we experience

the weird. I don't have the heart to
tell him I brought my own. Addie wants

to know what I'm going to do.
Oh, Addie, the night is young, the week

is young, and once so were we.
There are so many days yet to discover

what I'm going to do.

Adventure Awaits at Powell's City of Books

according to the sign.
They release the lions
into the poetry section,
daily at four o'clock p.m.

Meat Is Murder

There's a restaurant
at Third and Washington
called *Killer Burger*. I want
to walk in there and yell
THAT'S RIGHT!

Sleepless

We discover they have beds in Portland
just like they did in Seattle. The city has

streets and donuts. I have yet to count
all the bridges. TV tells me Dale Cooper

is the mayor. It's an easy transition for us.
I won't tell you what the man was yelling

in the street on the way to dinner. Ask me
privately. For the rest of you, *dog* was the

only friendly word. We had a dinner like
the kings and queens of Peru.

Half way to the donut shop a woman
stopped us with the words *you cannot be*

such a beautiful couple. This is my mother,
isn't she beautiful? – Of course she is, we tell

her. Who isn't, when you think about it?
When you peel away the unspeakable

words. When you lay in your bed with
all the plans made, and only eight hours

of sleep preventing you from getting to
them. *Alexa, can you still hear me?*

Portland
Day 1

Good Morning Portland

I misread the bottle in the hotel bathroom
that says *Geranium Conditioner* as

German Conditioner. Needless to say
my hair goes unconditioned today.

Good morning Portland!
All your beautiful mistakes

await me!

Keep Portland Weird

I wanted to go up to the *Just Chicken* food pod and ask for anything else. But I miss my opportunity because Addie told me my fly was down and I got into a whole thing where instead of zipping it up I just lifted my arms in the air and shouted *keep Portland weird!*

No

The man outside of Powell's books
with the hair, and the tie-dyed shirt
and the card that said *yes*.
Solidarity is expressed, *Yes!* I say.
Disappointed, he answers *It's just
words*, and I am forced to take my
yes home, no new bond in place.

Elevator Operator Needed

The Wells Fargo Center in downtown Portland has found a way to make elevator technology more complicated and less intuitive. Congratulations!

I Forget Whether It's Salmon or Trout That Spawn

We walk up Salmon Street to spawn...
Wait a minute is that trout?
Where is Trout Street?

Don't Go Here Because It's Nowhere

We walked quite a distance
to a museum that doesn't exist.
The Museum of the City,
a web only museum, the fine print
tells us, despite the physical address
elsewhere in the page.

A Woman walking through Pioneer Square

with a cold brew in one hand, and a fork in the other. She's ready to caffeinate or stab. Be wary, oh citizens of downtown. Anything can happen.

Thoughts of Jude Invade Our Vacation

They say Pioneer Square is *Portland's living room*. They haven't installed the couches yet, but already I can see our son leaving his socks on them all night long.

Things Learned, Said or Overheard on the Portland Walking Tour

I
Our guide straightens the furniture
in the waiting room. *Keep the ottomans weird*
I declare.

II
Pioneer square is the
number 4 best square
in the world, according
to someone who
rates squares.

III
The man who exposed himself
to the naked statue on 6th Avenue
was soon elected mayor.
The original hipster
(Bud Clark)

IV
At a certain point
Portland's citizens moved
to the suburbs and ate
casserole and Jello molds.

V
At Water Avenue Coffee
the employees get
health insurance.
So there's happiness
and love in their coffee.

VI
Conversation between tour guide and woman in wheel chair on the street.

W: Where do I catch the 9 bus?
G: I'm not positive.
W: No one in Portland is.
G: Well if you just walk across the street.
W: I'm crippled! I can't walk!
G: Well if you go across the street
you'll find the MET office.
W: No-one there will know any more
than you because they're fucking ignorant
because they're from Oregon!

VII
A state law says if you depict
a beaver in public art you also
have to depict a duck.

VIII
In cold weather they'll
sweater bomb the public art.

IX
Grace spends most of the tour
walking backwards. Somehow she
knows where she's going but only
sees where she's been.

X
Grace focuses a lot on the statues
with nudity for our benefit and
attention maintenance.

XI
They put in less comfortable chairs
at the bus stops because people used
to fall asleep waiting for their buses
sitting in the old, more comfy ones.
There was an epidemic of people
falling asleep waiting for buses.

XII
The creatively named *The Portland Building*
was named the 25th ugliest building in the world.
Most of the others on the list are in North Korea.

XIII
The Lady Portlandia
forged in copper
is the 50 ft woman
I've been looking for.

XIV
The park block was designed after the prompt
a cathedral of trees with a simple floor of grass.

XV
Portland was called *Stumptown*
because of what was left when
they cleared the trees to
make the town.

XVI
Portland was named after
Portland, Maine after a coin toss against
another guy who wanted to name it
Boston.

XVII
Boston, MA isn't aware of the rivalry
it has with Portland, OR that Portland
demonstrates with its Portland Cream
Donuts with eyes on then to demonstrate
that Portland has vision.

XVIII
No tree orgy ensues in the middle of the street
which separates the male only and female only
section of Chapman Square which houses
the sexually appropriate trees.

XIX
The state flag
is double sided
because they couldn't
give up the beaver.

XX
It's not a *three mountain day.*

XXI
We end the tour in one of
the two hearts of Portland.
Like a Time Lord Grace says
which makes us appreciate
her all the more.

Flipping Out

Dinner with Flip,
our friend from
the sacred place.

Tales are told of
naked bicycle rides
of missing poopers.

We eat and sing without
singing. We talk of
the clan of the butt.

Knowing there's a Flip
in Portland makes this
a city worth living in.

Sleepless

I had a sandwich for breakfast this morning made out of donuts and smoked gouda and arugula, and a fried egg. It's ruined other menus for me. I'm looking at what would otherwise be respectable options and thinking *yeah but it's not the Apple Frittwich.* In the mean time I keep threatening to leave the room for late night pizza or a midnight donut. They used to put medicine in the donuts here but stopped out of regulation or sensibility. They tell us the famous donuts are not the good ones. They tell us the coffee is better at the coffee shops. They tell us the government must spend money on art, and plastic bags are a luxury. City of bridges. City of roses. City of many sister cities. How many things can a city be of? My legs and feet will be willing to be told more things tomorrow. As for this exact moment, this mattress and these sheets, are all they need.

Portland
Day 2

Taking a Shower in the Hotel with Rick Lupert

I
Oolong tea in the shampoo?
What's next, hotel? Jus au bacon
in the conditioner? Voodoo Doughnuts
in the body wash? Portland finds ways
to combine things to make the day go
quicker, while I'm just at the beginning
and want it to last all day long.

II
Because the bottles look similar
I'm pretty sure I just shampooed
my left leg.

Smoothie, Donut, Coffee

We stop at three different places for breakfast because there are so many experiences to have and so little time.

Smoothie

They serve mango cheeks at *Kure* on 12th
which just seems kind of cruel to the mango.

Donut

Addie's eyes sparkle with sin as she pulls the two Blue Star Donut samples towards her. She's already had acai this morning so crimes against health and sensibility will now be committed. I look forward to seeing her photo on wanted posters at juice bars all over Portland.

Coffee

Stumptown Coffee at the Ace Hotel –
a hipsters paradise.

Served in mugs, at our request.
Finally a good cup of the sacred

beverage inside us. Fuel for
looking at art, for walking miles

and miles, for being as awake as
this city needs us to be.

Coffee-side Attraction

Addie makes me go into the bathroom in Stumptown Coffee, not because she feels I need to go or I have something that needs to be cleaned off, but because it has never ending tile ceiling to wall to floor to ceiling to wall. So I walk in, close the door behind me and do nothing in that space for a moment except enjoy the never ending...

The Weird Streets of Weird Portland

I
We pass by a store called *Portland Nap*
which I guess is like a hotel or something.

II
We pass by a food cart called *Potatoes on Ninth*...
I ask if they can put them on a plate instead.

III
There's a restaurant called *Elephants in the Park*
which is not true for many reasons.

IV
Two Portland weirdos
standing inside the flower bed
behind the sign that says
*Sensitive Plants, No People
Or Pets.*

At the Portland Art Museum

I
The Call to Arms
Auguste Rodin, 1879

Addie says that's a *crazy looking*
Angel and then gives a quiet scream
like a whispering Satan or she just
got a job as the lead singer for
Quiet Quiet Riot.

II
We see a sculpture of a duck
and wonder if there is a beaver
nearby as mandated by
Portland Law.

III
Only two rooms into the museum and already
a picture of me eating the hump of a camel.
Just two rooms into the museum and
we're all in.

IV
Addie wants to go everywhere she tells me
standing in front of *Ganesha Lord of Obstacles.*
(Pala Dynasty 750-1174)

Well we're already in Portland I tell her
which is a pretty good start.

V
The Lime Burner
James McNeill Whistler, 1859

Yes, burn all the limes James.
Burn them!

VI
Amboise
David Young Cameron, 1903

We see an etching of Amboise
drawn a hundred years before
our feet touched those
enchanting stones.

VII
Three Bad Guesses at
Chronos Clock
Adam Ferdinand Dietz (1708-1777)

It's Zeus.
It's Poseidon.
It's just a guy with a clock in his back.
(It's Chronos, Greek God of time.)

VIII
Chinoiserie door from the Ca' Rezzonico, Venice
Giovanni Domenici Tiepolo (maybe), 1760

This is what we need as our front door
Knock knock, *come in*
or just gaze at it forever.

IX
Bowl with Double Parrot Design
Korea, Goryeo Dynasty 12th/13th century

It's hard to see either parrot in this bowl.
But I now feel all works of art should be
labeled with the number of parrots they include.

X
The Circumcision of Christ
Jacob Cornelia's Van Oostsnanen, 1516

...is uncomfortably detailed.

XI
The Finding of Moses
Giovanni Battista Pittoni, 1739

...could also be called *The Finding of the Egyptian Princess's Nipple.* Miriam looks happy and since when were ancient Egyptians white?

XII
Allegory of Poetry
Jean-François de Troy, 1733

...could also be called
*If I keep writing, my nipples
will come out, and here comes
a Pegasus flying in to see them.*

XIII
The Game of Bowls
Pieter Angillis, 1727

...was a much simpler
and less deadly game than
the one of Thrones.

XIV
Group Portrait
Gabriel Revel, 1686

This one has everything –
a nipple, a puppy, naked baby angels,
a parrot. I'm pretty sure Jesus is hiding
behind one of the support columns.

XV
Two Roosters Fighting
Dirk Valkenburg, 1710

The dog is rooting
for Red.

XVI
Portrait of a Young Woman
Erastus Salisbury Field, 1830

It looks like they stuck another face
on this young woman – Perhaps that
of a young man.

XVII
Nydia, the Blind Flower Girl of Pompeii
Randolph Rogers, 1855/1844

What Addie whispers into her ear
I'll never know.

XVIII
Description in the Margot Grant Walsh Collection

I can't read anything that begins
The social, political and economic turmoil
as that just describes every place at
every time.

XIX
Ladle, sterling silver, 1925

That's a ladle! Addie says
You'll have to imagine a really
impressive ladle, and being
taken by it.

XX
Portrait of Annette Kaufman, 1932
Portrait of Louis Kaufman, 1927
Milton Avery

It tells you something that they had
to be in two separate paintings.

XXI
La Femme Assise (Seated Woman)
Ellie Nadelman, 1918-1921

This was back before they could
afford to put faces on things.

XXII
The Black Hat
Julian Alden Weir, 1900

Sure there's the hat –
But no mention of the
woman it sits on, or the
gentle strokes needed
for us to see her.

XXIII
Every time Addie sees something she likes –
an ancient tea set, a ceremonial frog headdress –
I motion to an imagined museum associate to
come and *wrap this up for us*. Addie is
wondering who I'm talking to or why
my credit card is out.

XXIV
Ladle
Tlingit, 19th Century

Now THIS is a ladle
she says, taking back
what she said about
the lesser ladle in the
previous room. I don't
know how much more
room for ancient ladles
I have in my suitcase.

XXV
Rattlesnake Basket
Unknown Mission Indian artist, 1909

Rattlesnake not included.

XXVI
If you're reading this poem it means
I've made the unfortunate decision of
including it in this book:

Why don't they have art
in museum bathrooms
I wonder, as I make my own.

XXVII
Seated Figure
Mexico, Veracruz, 809-1200

Addie and I show
how to drink coffee
when you have mugs
attached to your shoulders
in an unscheduled and
unofficial demonstration.

XXVIII
An exposed nipple in every room –

One of the museum's
founding principles.

XXIX
Den Meso (young girl)
Ronna Neurnschwander, 1986

The young girl
with thirteen spoons
sticking out of her chest
is a champion
cereal eater.

XXX
Horse of 1000 Hands III
Adrian Arleo, 2007

Make that 1002 when
Addie shows up and
gets involved.

XXXI
Combat Paper

They turn retired military uniforms
into paper upon which you can
write poetry in case the soldiers
have forgotten how.

XXXII
Nymphéas
Claude Monet, 1914-15

Addie and Monet meet again in Portland.
I've always had a feeling about those two.
I still have feelings for those two.

XXXIII
Le Petit Pâtissier
Chaïm Soutine, 1921

The little pastry cook
makes little pastries
for little people
like little me.

XXXIV
Despite the fact there is
so much more art to see
and so much more of
my life to get to
I hate leaving rooms
with Monets in them.

XXXV
Factories at Night
Joseph Stella, 1936/43

Pow pow pow!
Addie adds sound effects
    to the painting,
an imagined gun fight
behind rays of light
under a cloudy sky.

XXXVI
Bathers, Coney Island
Milton Avery, 1934

Man with pickle nose
sitting on a woman
is probably not what
Avery had in mind —
but here I am.

XXXVII
Tactual Stimulation Pink
Dafna Kaffeman, 2007

Addie is confident they
put these behind glass just so
she couldn't touch them.

XXXVIII
Quadruplets, New Orleans
Gloria Baker Feinstein, 2015

Three dressed the same
One the rebel with the striped dress
One with the black shoes
One with the belt and the fan and
    the hidden lips
One with the bracelet who
    didn't have time to do anything
    with her hair.

XXXIX
The Means to an End...A Shadow Drama in Five Acts
Kara Walker, 1995

1
Large child breastfeeds
while defying gravity

2
Wolf steals
little girl

3
Eventually they
form a dance troupe

4
Meanwhile
disembodied head
in snowstorm

5
Fat Abraham Lincoln
to the rescue!

At the Cafe Behind The Museum

There is a staff changeover while we eat
so people we don't know say *goodbye*
when we leave. Yes, *goodbye*,
whoever you people are.

At *Farm Spirit*

Rico says *drinking vinegar*
like that's a thing.

Violent Femmes and
Love and Rockets –

I'm pretty sure
I went to high school with Rico.

No one was embarrassed when
they served the *naked asparagus*.

This is the second dinner in Portland
I weep at the end of.

Found Truth

They say
at Voodoo Doughnut
the magic is in the hole.
This has also always been
my philosophy.

At Sizzle Pie

I
Sizzle Pie has a pizza
called the *Uncle Beef*.
I'm more looking for the
Aunt Tomato.

II
At Sizzle Pie they say
Death to False Pizza!
and I say give me the uniform –
I will fight for your cause!
(which is my cause)

III
At Sizzle Pie the restrooms
are for customers only
so what choice did we have really?
this is the wisdom of pizza
at ten o'clock in the evening.

End of Night Traditions

Walk a hundred miles (hyperbole)
Consider late night food (could go either way)
Pass through hotel doors (it's the only way)
Receive acknowledgement from hoteliers (keeps us coming back)
Drink from the fruit water fountain (it exists)
State lack of desire to go to fitness room (resistance is futile)
Manipulate things in fitness room (runs in the family)
Determine if elevators can talk (some do)
Remove shoes in room (feet grateful)
Plan tomorrow (most time spent on breakfast)
Remove everything else (let there be no obstruction)
Sleep until the locally sourced cows come home (moo)

New Tradition

Last night both Addie and I separately knocked the iron off the ironing board in the middle of the night. So tonight I offered to pre-throw it to the floor before we went to bed just to save us the time later.

One Poorly Constructed, Too Long Sentence

It just so happened that the one time a day the Hawthorne Bridge lifts, blocking humans, cars, and bicycles (come to think of it humans are involved with cars and bicycles), so a boat can pass through, or so the weights will stay in working order, was the exact time, today, we were walking across it, only to be stopped by the railroad gate-like arms, and the blinking red sign, and the yellow line painted on the sidewalk, as we digested our thirty-six course dinner (every time I speak of it, the number of courses goes up) and watched the sunset over the hills of Portland, and gazed longingly at the other bridges, including the pedestrian-only one, which is the newest, and which reminds us of the Millennium Bridge in London which is in England, where the first Portland is, that all the Portlands are named after, including the one in Maine, and the one we're about to sleep a third night in, in the great state of Oregon which is like a west coast Vermont, holler if you know what I mean, and like this sentence which has gone on too long, *this* sentence, and our day, are now over.

Portland
Day 3

Good Morning Portland

Whenever we pass by the Paris Metro map
on Washington Street, which is every day as we
walk up to 12th Street, a Mecca for breakfast,
my French accent comes out and says
something like *ahh Paris,* and pretty
shortly we're walking by the store that
has the word *Bubois* in its name which
I've personally decided is Portland French
for *boobies*, except for this morning when
I'm a little tired and don't say *bubois*
out loud, but we're at the point where
Addie expects it, and breakfast will not
happen until she gets a *bubois* out of me.
So I say it and even though it sounds a
little forced Addie is satisfied, and a biscuit
and eggs can now happen. Good morning
Portland. We're getting it all figured out.

At Tasty n Alder

I
The waitress asks if
I want to hold on
to my fork.
I'm not sure if
it's a subtle suggestion
or if she just wants to
take it away.

II
The *Portlandia* TV show theme comes
on while we eat. Finally! I have to
specify *TV show* as long before
Fred and Carrie there was Portland's
goddess, invented for this city
keeping us safe from music-less
breakfasts and all things normal.

III
Addie's having a moment with her latte.
It may be the homemade almond milk
or the skillfully rendered foam design
or the word *heart* on the mug.
In any case I'm going to have to up my
game. *It's a nice treat with the espresso*
she says. *You're a nice treat* I say
looking into her eyes. Oh, it's on.

At Washington Park

The bus that takes you around the park had that new shuttle smell.

At the Japanese Garden

I
*What do you think the policy is
on pants* I wonder out loud which
leads to a whole extra layer of
security developed just for me.

II
The little Japanese girl
with the sneakers that squeak
like a squeaky toy
every time she takes a step
add an extra special element
to the rock garden.

III
Puff the Magic Dragon
but in Japanese plays in the
Japanese Garden Gift Shop

IV
Photobombing poseurs
introduces us to Sherman Oaks locals.
We should have carpooled.

V
Addie hands me one
kitten flipbook after another.
She knows just what
to hand me.

VI
You'd think I would have
written more haiku in the
Japanese garden

In the Rose Test Garden

I
Smell my pink flamingo
a little girl says to her brother
or future husband
with context I'll never know.

II
At the Rose Test Garden
we stop and smell the roses –
All of them.

III
A woman named Rose
is walking through the
rose garden with a
particular sense of
entitlement.

IV
A toddler screams a war cry
then runs around a a tree
in the Shakespeare Garden.
He wins the day.

V
Addie's voice goes up
several octaves as she
reacts to her encounter
with the miniature roses.

VI
Our timing has us miss the start
of the ballet practice but we hear
the music begin in the distance so
I perform what I would imagine to be
the routine for Addie who does not
verbally acknowledge her assessment
but her wide eyes tell me everything.

Hair on the Tram

The man on the tram tells his little boy many interesting and educational things except how not to have a mullet.

Coffee

I
I walked in to Public Domain Coffee
and claimed I had the copyright.

II
You can't walk three feet in Portland
without tripping over a coffee shop.

The Kimpton Hotel Monaco Portland is the Best Hotel in the World

Free *Voodoo Doughnuts* as part
of the Kimpton wine hour.
No standing in line.
We are literally the
kings of the world.

P.S. That is not the correct use of the word *literally*.

Bus to Alberta Street

Man gets on with a Creamsicle
Can't be legal.

Addie and I sit separately
due to available seats.

She sees my face across the bus
the recently departed wine hour in my eyes.

Clear Portland skies try to convince us
it never rains.

Traffic across the bridge
reminds us of home.

Girl two seats over is in a world
fueled by her headphones.

We communicate across the aisle
by moving our lips.

We say nothing
and everything.

We drive across the weighted draw bridge.
When I was a child, I drew a bridge.

In the middle of the bridge, Addie's lips pucker.
This is what we do over water.

The temperature in the bus is different
from the temperature outside.

Addie bonds with Los Angeles transplants.
Portland draws us like magnets.

Our stop is either close or far.
This is the limit of our knowledge.

People keep getting on the bus
But no one gets off. This can't go in forever.

Captain Underpants is playing at a theatre outside.
I knew him when he was a corporal.

A boy from Paris talks with a girl from Japan.
He is sad she's never been to Paris.

Our bus driver is the best bus driver.
We can tell.

I want to pull to signal our stop but everyone
is going where we are going.

Portland houses look like
Portland houses.

The angry woman texting
at the bus bench at Fremont.

The Thai restaurant the man
from yesterday told me about.

Last Thursday on Alberta

I
About *Random Order Pie Bar*
on Alberta Street:
Ahh the convenience of
not having to make a decision.

II
We walk by *Little Big Burger*.
I yell in the door *make a decision!*

III
I misread words on a T-shirt
that says *Spread da Love* as
Spread Dracula.

IV
Barbershop for rent.
Barbers not included

V
It's Halloween
every *Last Thursday*
on Alberta Street.

VI
We pass three *Vitas* on Alberta Street
as we walk through, apparently,
the Vita district.

VII
Flip tells us
more tales of the
naked bike ride.

VIII
If I had a big hammer
where would I keep it?
(inside a big toolbox)

IX
I like the empty booth
with a sign on it that says
Free 5 Day Trial.

X
One sign says *More than just ribs.*
But I didn't have any expectations
to begin with

XI
I wanted to take a picture
by the sign that said *Lickety*
but my tongue has been out
too much on this trip already.

XII
The woman with the
Let's get weird t-shirt –
I'm all in lady.

Bus Ride Home

And by *home* I mean the place
with the party in the lobby.

The family who asked for money
to ride the bus, is on the bus.

The tie-dyed couple –
beards and hats to match.

Earlier today I saw a *Chipotle*
in the distance.

The coughing man will
be the death of us.

He is a situation.
His coughs like clockwork.

We cross another bridge.
I've lost count of all the bridges.

Our stop is coming but
does it ever really stop?

Sleepless

Two doughnuts and a shot of American Whiskey
are all that remain of our last night in Portland

Our last night of this thirteenth honeymoon
Our last night of only having the responsibility

to feed ourselves. And we have fed ourselves...
the scale at home awaits us with its number of

judgement. Our cats at home await us with
their nonchalant looks of *oh, were you gone?*

Our pile of mail, our peaches, our light switches.
Soon it will be time to celebrate our bathroom's

first birthday. Soon my body will be placed in
the work chair. But there are hours to go.

A foreign bed ready to wrap itself around me.
A half a day to pretend it's not over.

A breakfast, a reunion, points to be collected
for checking in. Then a train to the airport.

A flight...I'd list it all but my eyes are so heavy now.
I can't lift them. I'm going to give in to gravity.

It's already won.

Portland to Los Angeles

At Cheryl's on 12th

I will be the second person I know of
wearing a *Millennium Falcon* t-shirt
in Portland, today. Maybe more if I
come across a mirror.

We're returning to the scene of the
breakfast crime. And by *crime*, I mean
we enjoyed it so much, it should
be illegal.

Another poet encounter – She's promised
to get her buns out early for us. I like
to take things literally, so this morning
has so much potential.

The Special Condition of Poets

We meet with Mindy and discuss,
among other things, the special
condition of poets, which is a thing
that had always previously been
unsaid, but which couldn't be more
obvious now that it's appeared out loud.

Later we take in a *Case Study* of coffee
across the street from the library offering
a view of homeless streaming into the
front doors where, we assume, they are
not allowed to continue their screams.

I think there is a certain style here I
can only describe as *Portland Sexy*.
Sometimes it involves beards, but
mostly it's a mixture of black and
what is revealed when the sun comes out.

It feels like you could really exist as a human
here. *They really know how to interact,* Addie
says, and I'm already planning where we'd
live and which methods of public transportation
I would take from one place to the next.

This is the longest last day, a symptom of
never leaving the west coast. Soon enough
our feet will touch the ground in Burbank,
California and our attentions will shift to
what furniture to put in the backyard as

we continue this idyllic life, under the
immigrant palm trees of our neighborhood
accepting deliveries of packages in two
days or less, imagining another summer
in another place on the other side of the fence.

Millennials

I normally don't take off my clothes for strangers
I tell the man seated outside of Cheryl's on 12th
wearing a Millennium Falcon t-shirt in front of
three other people I assume are his friends as I
unzip my orange hoody to reveal the same t-shirt
wrapped around my torso to the quick relief of
the seated party who wasn't sure what was about
to happen, and how far I was about to go to.
Keep Portland Weird.

At Case Study Coffee

The barista tells us he roasted the beans himself so even if we don't like the coffee, at least we know it's for real.

Yamhill

The street Yamhill is
indeed on a hill otherwise
it feels like a deception.

Also I'm renaming all
the streets in Los Angeles
Yamhill.

haiku

When giving a hug
no one squeezes tighter than
Mindy Nettifee

P.S. This is an authentic haiku because
Mindy Nettifee occurs in nature.

Downtown

One-way streets make it
a lot easier not to die
when you choose to
cross the street before
the light has changed.

Can't Swarm

The social network has decided, early in the day, I don't deserve coins for being places. Their algorithm has no idea who I am or what I am doing.

Decombuttssion

Addie spends so little time
in the shoe store, my butt hardly
has time to compress the cushion
of the non-shoe buying spouse couch.

I'm Famous

When I didn't see any copies of my books
on the shelves of *Powell's City of Books*
I assumed they had sold out and were having
difficulty keeping them in stock and felt
really great about myself.

Brendan is Famous

When I didn't see a copy of your book
on the shelf at *Powell's City of Books*
even though the in-house search system
said it would be there, I assumed it had been
stolen and that you would love the street cred
implied with that.

Leaving the Kimpton

They finally change the fruit in the
water infusers on the day we leave.
I guess they assumed we were
more melon people.

I Learn I Am Garbage

My last interaction with a native Portlander
at the MET stop to the airport, who rams into

standing-still me with his walker.
I ask if he wants me to move

and he answers *yeah garbage,*
and then gets in the train.

Farewell Portland...I almost got out
unscathed. One more story to tell.

Train Ride to the Airport

People and their luggage
Leaving home or going home

Skidmore Fountain sounds like
Skateboard Mountain

A pulled emergency knob
The small delays

The doors are closing but
the doors are already closed

A man's fist and a yellow pole
A tired dog's face

Our dogs are tired
I left my waterfall in the north

I'm experiencing a burrito deficiency
Electronic check-in isn't possible

I see mountains or clouds
Or clouds of mountains

Goodbye sleeping dog
Goodbye sleeping girl

Goodbye army of text messagers
Goodbye weird

The new normal
The air I want to breathe

On the Airplane

I
The 5 freeway is packed in Portland.
Both ways! I'm glad we're flying home.

II
This long distance thing
isn't working out
I mean, out-of-state cheese?
What was I thinking?
says the airline magazine
which now has me questioning
every relationship I've ever had
with cheese.

III
We are number one for departure.
It feels good to have status of
some kind.

IV
Washington has had
more Sasquatch sightings
than any other state
says the airline magazine.
We didn't see him, but
I hear he summers in
Vera Cruz with Chupacabra.

Los Angeles

I
I misread the sign in Burbank Airport
that says *Check-In* as *Chicken*.
Ahh brain and eyes, we'll always
have Portland.

II
Los Angeles goes on forever
I think, as we take the long ride home
passing by streets that never end.

About The Author

The author, anxious in Portland

Two-time Pushcart Prize, and Best of the Net nominee Rick Lupert has been involved with poetry in Los Angeles since 1990. He was awarded the Beyond Baroque Distinguished Service Award in 2014 for service to the Los Angeles poetry community. He served for two years as a co-director of the non-profit literary organization Valley Contemporary Poets. His poetry has appeared in numerous magazines and literary journals, including *The Los Angeles Times, Rattle, Chiron Review, Red Fez, Zuzu's Petals, Stirring, The Bicycle Review, Caffeine Magazine, Blue Satellite* and others. He edited the anthologies *A Poet's Siddur: Shabbat Evening - Liturgy Through the Eyes of Poets, Ekphrastia Gone Wild - Poems Inspired by Art, A Poet's Haggadah: Passover through the Eyes of Poets,* and *The Night Goes on All Night - Noir Inspired Poetry*, and is the author of twenty-two other books: *17 Holy Syllables, God Wrestler: A Poem for Every Torah Portion,* (Ain't Got No Press) *Donut Famine, Romancing the Blarney Stone, Professor Clown on Parade, Making Love to the 50 Ft. Woman, The Gettysburg Undress* (Rothco Press), *Nothing in New England is New, Death of a Mauve Bat, Sinzibuckwud!, We Put Things In Our Mouths, Paris: It's The Cheese, I Am My Own Orange County, Mowing Fargo, I'm a Jew. Are You?, Feeding Holy Cats, Stolen Mummies, I'd Like to Bake Your Goods, A Man With No Teeth Serves Us Breakfast* (Ain't Got No Press), *Lizard King of the Laundromat, Brendan Constantine is My Kind of Town* (Inevitable Press) and *Up Liberty's Skirt* (Cassowary Press), and the spoken word album *Rick Lupert Live and Dead* (Ain't Got No Press). He hosted the long running Cobalt Café reading series in Canoga Park for almost twenty-one years and has read his poetry all over the world.

Rick created and maintains *Poetry Super Highway*, an online resource and publication for poets (PoetrySuperHighway.com), *Haikuniverse*, a daily online small poem publication (Haikuniverse.com), and writes and occasionally draws the daily web comic *Cat and Banana* with Brendan Constantine. (facebook.com/catandbanana) He also writes the weekly Jewish poetry blog *From the Lupertverse* for JewishJournal.com

Currently Rick works as a music teacher at synagogues in Southern California and as a graphic and web designer for anyone who would like to help pay his mortgage.

Rick's Other Books and Recordings

17 Holy Syllables
Ain't Got No Press ~ January, 2018

A Poet's Siddur: Friday Evening (edited by)
Ain't Got No Press ~ November, 2017

God Wrestler: A Poem for Every Torah Portion
Ain't Got No Press ~ August, 2017

Donut Famine
Rothco Press ~ December, 2016

Romancing the Blarney Stone
Rothco Press ~ December, 2016

Professor Clown on Parade
Rothco Press ~ December, 2016

Rick Lupert Live and Dead (Album)
Ain't Got No Press ~ March, 2016

Making Love to the 50 Ft. Woman
Rothco Press ~ May, 2015

The Gettysburg Undress
Rothco Press ~ May, 2014

  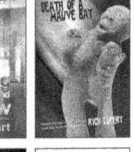

Ekphrastia Gone Wild (edited by)
Ain't Got No Press ~ July, 2013

Nothing in New England is New
Ain't Got No Press ~ March, 2013

Death of a Mauve Bat
Ain't Got No Press ~ January, 2012

The Night Goes On All Night Noir Inspired Poetry (edited by)
Ain't Got No Press ~ November, 2011

Sinzibuckwud!
Ain't Got No Press ~ January, 2011

We Put Things In Our Mouths
Ain't Got No Press ~ January, 2010

A Poet's Haggadah (edited by)
Ain't Got No Press ~ April, 2008

A Man With No Teeth Serves Us Breakfast
Ain't Got No Press ~ May, 2007

I'd Like to Bake Your Goods
Ain't Got No Press ~ January, 2006

Stolen Mummies
Ain't Got No Press ~ February, 2003

Brendan Constantine is My Kind of Town
Inevitable Press ~ September, 2001

Up Liberty's Skirt
Cassowary Press ~ March, 2001

Feeding Holy Cats
Cassowary Press ~ May, 2000

I'm a Jew, Are You?
Cassowary Press ~ May, 2000

Mowing Fargo
Sacred Beverage Press ~ December, 1998

Lizard King of the Laundromat
The Inevitable Press ~ February, 1998

I Am My Own Orange County
Ain't Got No Press ~ May, 1997

Paris: It's The Cheese
Ain't Got No Press ~ May, 1996

For more information:
www.PoetrySuperHighway.com

www.ingramcontent.com/pod-product-compliance
Lightning Source LLC
Chambersburg PA
CBHW071731080526
44588CB00013B/1982